Get Out of Jail Card

A journey of self-worth

Russell Sturgess

This first edition was published in Australia in 2018 by
EAP Publishing

PO Box 1043, Cotton Tree,
Queensland, Australia. 4558

Copyright © 2018 by Russell Sturgess

All rights reserved. No part of this book may be reproduced or utilised in any form or by any means, electronic or mechanical, without permission in writing from the publisher.

The author of this book does not dispense medical advice or prescribe the use of any technique as a form of treatment for physical, mental and emotional problems without the advice of a medical practitioner, either directly or indirectly. The intent of the author is only to offer information of a general nature to help you in your quest for mental, emotional, physical and spiritual wellbeing. In the event you use any of the information in this book for yourself, the author and the publisher assume no responsibility for your actions.

pbk - ISBN 13: 978-0-9806089-1-5
eBook - ISBN 13: 978-0-9806089-2-2

the author

Russell Sturgess was born in Queensland, Australia in 1958. From the age of 15 he was trained in Osteopathic Massage and went on to formal studies and clinical practice until the mid 90's.

In the 90's Russell taught a version of the Osteopathic Massage technique developed by Tom Bowen, that Russell called Fascial Kinetics. This was taught extensively throughout the USA, New Zealand and Australia.

During this time he studied Attitudinal Healing with Drs Gerry Jampolsky and Susan Trout in the USA. Since then, Russell has taught and expanded his understanding of how to live life with inner-peace through being aware and mindful. To help others do the same, Russell developed the Enhances Awareness Program (EAP).

content

dedication i

illustrations ii

acknowledgements iii

preface iv

Introduction The game of life 1

Chapter 1 The unintentional crime 7

Chapter 2 Your life sentence 21

Chapter 3 Life in jail 35

Chapter 4 Getting out of jail 47

Chapter 5 Out on parole 63

Chapter 6 Being pardoned 83

Afterword About EAP 99

dedication

dedicated to those
seeking the
alchemy of life

illustrations

author	Russell (age 58)
Page 3	Monopoly Board
Page 9	Adelaide Sturgess
Page 16	Russell (age 7)
Page 41	Russell (age 44)
Page 56	Russell (age 52)
Page 58	Monopoly Board
Page 65	Finisterre Boat Harbour
Page 69	Russell's Camino Scallop Shell
Page 70	Caldo Gallego Soup

All photos were taken by Russell Sturgess and modified using Sketch Photo App.

acknowledgements

I want to acknowledge all of the people who have trusted me to be their health practitioner, educator, mentor and colleague throughout the years. I have been privileged to positively impact the lives of many people during my journey, and in most instances what I offered was new and unfamiliar. It took a degree of courage to follow me into uncharted waters, but you did. To you all, I am extremely grateful.

When a movie depicts some form of cruelty to animals, it will clearly state that no animals have been hurt in the production of the film. It is with regret that I cannot say the same about the production of my life. That said, I want to acknowledge the people who have been put into a position where they could experience mental anguish or emotional suffering as a result of my lack of awareness. Being slow to grasp the concept of awareness and mindfulness meant that more people than necessary were put into this situation. To you all, I am deeply remorseful.

Finally, I want to acknowledge the three women (Sharon, Anna and Rosie) who have walked parts of this journey with me. Your presence in my life has been a blessing. I thank you for helping me better understand love.

preface

In 2014 I was invited to present a paper on my first book Metanoia, at a tarot conference in Keswick in the northwest of England. I was accommodated in a historical BnB called Greta Hall. It was originally the home of Samuel Taylor Coleridge, an English poet, philosopher and theologian, who along with William Wordsworth was a founder of the Romantic Movement in England. Earlier in 2014, I wrote the first draft of this book, which included Wordsworth's Ode, Intimations of Immortality.

The owners of Greta Hall told me my bedroom had originally been Coleridge's office, where he and Wordsworth would spend hours discussing their poetry, prose and philosophical observations. They lent me a copy of a book about the history of the home. As I flipped through the pages, I came across this entry taken from Coleridge's diary — "On 27 March 'William wrote part of an Ode.' This was Intimations of Immortality, which they took with them to Keswick the next day."

Here I was, sleeping in the room where this poem which resinated with me was first drafted by Wordsworth. I had goose bumps, and could hardly contain my delight. I read it again —

Our birth is but a sleep and a forgetting:
The Soul that rises with us, our life's Star
Hath had elsewhere its setting,
And cometh from afar:
Not in entire forgetfulness,
And not in utter nakedness,
But trailing clouds of glory do we come
From God, who is our home:
Heaven lies about us in our infancy!
Shades of the Jail-house begin to close
Upon the growing Boy,
But he beholds the light, and whence it flows,
He sees it in his joy;
The Youth, who daily farther from the east
Must travel, still is Nature's priest,
And by the vision splendid
Is on his way attended;
At length the Man perceives it die away,
And fade into the light of common day.
Earth fills her lap with pleasures of her own;
Yearnings she hath in her own natural kind,
And, even with something of a mother's mind,
And no unworthy aim,
The homely nurse doth all she can
To make her foster-child, her Inmate Man,
Forget the glories he hath known,
And that imperial palace whence he came.

William Wordsworth
from Ode - Intimations of Immortality (1802)

"We become so imprisoned by our story and our beliefs about who we think we need to be in order to feel love and acceptance, that we eventually let go of our dreams and spend our energy on working out how to survive."

Russell Sturgess

introduction

The game of life

Get Out of Jail Card

One of my fondest memories from my childhood was playing Monopoly with my brother, and family friends on a Sunday afternoon. Hours of 'keeping the sabbath-day holy' were transformed from boredom to contained relief as Rich Uncle Pennybags ushered us into the world of property and high finance. There were two cards from the Chance and Community Chest piles that we all feared most, 'Pay Taxes' and 'Go To Jail'.

These, along with their associated game-board tiles, would bring squeals of delight or anguish whenever they came into play. On several occasions, I spent more than my fair share of the game in jail. It was frustrating when others were buying up property, avoiding rent, and collecting $200 as they passed 'Go'. All the while I was struggling to throw doubles and was constantly missing turns.

As I think back over my life since those innocent days, the 'Monopoly of life' also insisted that I spend long periods of time in jail — fortunately not literally. My jail was one formed within my own mind. And, just like the Monopoly game, while I was in this jail, the rest of the world appeared to be playing the game of life free of constraint, accumulating money, buying up properties, all the while passing 'Go' and collecting $200. It was as if my life became 'Monopoly - The Hell Version'. In this version, every third Chance card was the 'Go to Jail' card and the dice were loaded, meaning

The game of life

doubles were almost impossible. It appeared that once you landed in jail, getting out was highly unlikely.

I've since found out that this version wasn't all hell. A 'Get Out of Jail' card does in fact exist. It is hidden in plain sight, yet difficult to find, and it appears that very few actually find it. In the real-life version of Monopoly, once learned, the special powers of the 'Get Out of Jail' card can last a lifetime.

I have come to realise that we have all been sent to jail. We have all been given a life sentence, not only for 25 years, a typical life sentence, but for many of us, 'for the

term of our natural lives'. These personal jails are built from the attitudes and beliefs, the fears and the expectations, which frame almost every choice we make throughout life.

Our life sentence emerges from our personal narrative, a story of sorts, that took form though our early childhood. The forms that these mental prisons take are numerous and, in the game of life, can manifest as soulless employment, unemployment, abusive relationships, divorce and separation, debt, bankruptcy, loneliness, depression, anxiety and addiction. Most inmates aren't even aware that they are serving a life sentence, which resulted in imprisonment. Even when they get an inkling and try to escape, not understanding what got them there in the first place drags them back into their story once again, inevitably locking them back in their self-imposed imprisonment.

How do you know if you are in jail?

Besides the list of challenging life experiences described above, there are other ways to tell if you are in jail, or not — mental clarity, wellbeing, a sustained sense of joy and freedom from limiting fears.

What you experience inside the jail is 'not-stillness'. When you experience a feeling, thought or emotion to which you

The game of life

attribute a meaning, conscious or otherwise, this indicates that you are in jail. Anytime you are experiencing a feeling, thought or emotion, through which you maintain your awareness, and to which you give no meaning, then you are free of your life sentence — no longer imprisoned. In this place you maintain stillness.

In jail, you get caught up in your thoughts and feelings. You might have experienced waking in the middle of the night, swamped by thoughts of overwhelming scarcity (e.g. not enough money, not enough love). That is a common experience of 'not-stillness' — not having inner peace.

The object of this book is to help you identify your particular life sentence, your story. It will also assist you in applying for parole; releasing yourself from imprisonment; serving out your parole and then enjoying the freedom of being pardoned. Being pardoned will mean your life will be lived with a deep sense of self-worth. You will live with clarity of purpose and, through that, fulfilment.

I was in a personal jail most of my life. I went through divorce and struggled with stable relationships. I was burnt-out, depressed, addicted and bankrupt. Sadly, living life from my jail meant that I had, both intentionally and unintentionally, hurt people. With hindsight, I sincerely regret that I was unaware.

Get Out of Jail Card

A great teacher of awareness explained that when you love much, much is forgiven. Enhanced awareness, the consciousness required to live life mindfully, is the highest expression of love that makes forgiveness possible. By being more consistently aware, you develop empathy, and from empathy, compassion and from compassion, benevolence. This is as much for yourself as it is for others. Inner stillness is what naturally arises from awareness, forgiveness and being mindful.

I have been released from my personal jail, evidenced by more frequent moments of stillness. Sure, I have more to do and am still working through my parole conditions. But I am a free man having worked out what it takes to be released from my prison. You can also be free. This little book is your guide to finding your 'Get Out of Jail' card.

chapter 1

The unintentional crime

Get Out of Jail Card

The unintentional crime from which we get our life sentence (our story) begins before our birth. We are each born into, and with, a unique collection of circumstances, which forms the rare blueprint of consciousness that bears our name. We are a conglomeration of inherited human DNA (from our biological parents); direct and indirect infant programming (from those who raise us and our culture); and the consequences of personal experience (from our life's journey). As Wordsworth suggested, there is also a fourth aspect. 'The Soul that rises with us, our life's Star, Hath had elsewhere its setting, And cometh from afar.'

Like a kaleidoscope with its multi-faceted filters, the view we have of life is distorted by our personal filters. These filters were crafted from the blending of our soul's agenda, the chemistry which formed us into matter, the understanding of life that we individually accrued through our programming, and the pains and joys experienced through living life. Let me illustrate.

Our chemistry

My youngest daughter, Adelaide, was born with missing chromosomes which resulted in her developing a set of symptoms that are collectively referred to as William's Syndrome. This anomaly in her DNA is a fundamental part

The unintentional crime

of the filter that causes her to see life differently to most people. A common characteristic of William's is an overly friendly nature. Everywhere Adelaide goes in her community people know and engage with her. She knows more people than I do.

As her primary carer from the age of 12, I encouraged Adelaide to actively participate in life and to go and do things independently. So, when she was of 'legal' age, she went night clubbing on her own. She joined a church group of her choice, and for several years lived independently.

Part of Adelaide's filter is her intellectual disability. With limited literacy and numeracy skills, Addy (as she is fondly known) learnt to trust the advice and recommendations of other people in order to move 'safely' through life. Addy became adept at scanning the faces of people for the subtlest of nuances that would help her decide if they could be trusted, or not.

Like Addy, our DNA is significant in building the filters for how we see life.

Our programming

I recall the story of a truly beautiful young woman who felt it necessary to actively encourage young men to engage with her sexually in an attempt to gain approval. Why was it that someone so attractive resorted to acting out so recklessly?

It turned out that her mother, who was also beautiful, would regularly look at herself in a mirror and, with her young daughter looking on, criticise the reflection. She was unintentionally programming her daughter to believe that what was beautiful could be perceived as ugly. The daughter indeed believed she was ugly and felt she had to be promiscuous to get attention. The behaviours of the mother helped to form her daughter's filter. Recently Dove® posted a YouTube video that highlighted the way a mother's attitude can mould the attitude of her daughter. Look up the Dove® Mother/Daughter Experiment.

Our familial programming filters the way we engage with life.

Our experience

Cynophobia is the name given to someone who has a fear of dogs. It is one of the world's most prevalent phobias, typically arising from either direct or indirect frightening experiences with dogs. It is common for someone who has been bitten by a dog at an early age to maintain a life-long fear. In spite of how irrational this behaviour might appear to someone with no fear, the fact remains, their experience forms the filter that has them believe all dogs are dangerous.

Our life experience is the third way we build the filters which give meaning to our life.

Our soul's agenda

The idea that the soul carries blueprints integrated into our personal filters has been a belief strongly held by various cultures throughout history. That heavenly bodies (astrology) can play a part in the formation of individual filters might be a challenging concept for some people.

I have personally studied and consulted as a Numerologist for over 30 years. Numerology uses numbers from birth dates to identify personal filters. There is empirical evidence of how Numerology reveals individual characteristics and preferences, which manifest in the nature of a child from birth.

Wordsworth suggested that, '…our soul that rises with us

hath had elsewhere its setting, and cometh from afar'. Numerology and Astrology are tools for capturing a glimpse of the soul's journey.

If you believe in an eternal soul, or reincarnation, the soul's journey affects the way we filter in this life.

The crime is committed

The majority of the filters that a person uses to interpret life's experiences are established by the age of seven. I would like you to take a moment to consider what was going on in your life during your first seven years:

Where was your family living?

Did you have younger or older siblings?

What work did your parents do?

What was the state of your parent's emotional, mental and physical health, especially your mother?

What was your family's socio-economic status?

What was your nature as a child?

What attitudes and beliefs did your mother hold about herself? And your dad?

What was the state of your health?

What are your most significant early childhood recollections?

The unintentional crime

Were you traumatised as a child?
Was your childhood joyful?

The answers to many of these questions will help you to understand the nature of the filters you've created and bring to your life experience as an adult. (As I write this, Harry Chapin is singing Cats in the Cradle 'And as I hung up the phone it occurred to me, He'd grown up just like me, My boy was just like me...'). The filters that emerged from our formative years resulted in a personal story that is responsible for populating our lives with the people and the experiences that we encounter along the way.

Real life stories

Here are examples from real-life stories that highlight some of the jails people create for themselves (names have been changed for obvious reasons).

Brian

Brian was born into circumstances where both parents worked and both were alcoholics. From a very young age he was left on his own, right from grade one he would come home to an empty house. He had older siblings, but they were out and about with their friends. Brian found solace in watching TV and did little to socialise. This trend continued throughout his formative years.

Now in his 60's, Brian still doesn't have many friends, and any social life is mostly initiated by his partner. He spends hours every day watching documentaries and movies on TV. Brian struggles to know how to relate to people because it was never modelled. As a mature adult, Brian is depressed, unemployed, struggles with his weight and health, and lives almost as a recluse. The crime in Brian's childhood was one of omission.

Linda

Linda was the child of Christian missionaries working in a remote 'native' mission during the 60's. She was sexually abused as a young child by locals who worked for her parents. Although she reported the incident to her parents, no action was taken and the abuse continued.

Linda's disdain for men, and fear of dark skinned men, became a key theme throughout her life. She became fearful of most men she encountered. She allowed herself to trust only one man. He became her protector and husband. She has lived a tightly controlled life, a life imprisoned by her fear.

The unintentional crime

Sally

Sally grew up watching her mother work hard. Her mum was so driven to try to prove her usefulness, she would walk in the door after work and not even remove her coat. Instead she immediately commenced the house work, and prepared the evening meal. Sally's mum was often awake until midnight doing chores and then be up early, doing more chores before heading off to work. Consequently, Sally spent a lot of time in her formative years with her grandmother, who repeatedly told her that her mother would never be good at anything, and was useless, no matter how hard she worked.

Now in her 40's, Sally doesn't get to bed before midnight and works at a frantic pace each day. In addition, she studies and does research in order to prove that she is both useful and good at something.

We each have our own version of these themes. The good news is, as an adult we can break away from the programming that emerged through our childhood.

My story

I was born in November 1958. During that year my dad was living 80 kilometres away, six days a week, while he built his new business. Two months before my birth my mum and two older siblings moved to permanently join him. In 1957, my mum went full term with her third pregnancy and gave birth to a girl who lived less than 24 hours.

Without the assistance that is available to women today who find themselves in similar circumstances, she faced enormous personal challenges and depression. Remember, she was on her own with two young boys six days a week.

To help resolve her depression, her doctor suggested having another child, which was me! Then, about six months after my birth, my mother fell pregnant once more and gave birth to a six-week premature baby who required lots of nurturing. It isn't hard to imagine the stress she was experiencing over that two-year period. Three pregnancies, a death, moving home, living in a new town, and a child in need of extra care. This was the physical and emotional environment of my first 12 months.

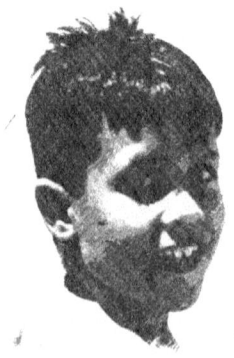

Through my formative years I established my position in the family in a way that made sure I wasn't overlooked. My eldest brother was eight years my senior and possessed the older sibling authority and

The unintentional crime

strength. My other brother was five years my senior and he possessed intelligence. Given my age and size I couldn't compete with either one and had to find my own way to be of value. On reflection, I developed emotional astuteness and became 'the sensitive one'.

Where my older brothers established their worth through athletic prowess and academic achievement respectively, I became involved in the performing arts and enrolled in various community service groups. By 15, I had learnt massage and quickly worked out that I could establish my worth through helping people feel better. Through performing arts, community service and healing, I found a way to feel good about myself. I also sought the attention of girls, and had a steady girlfriend by the age of 15.

From my childhood, I emerged with a sense that I was overlooked. If I could find a way to help people feel better, I would be noticed and, if I was noticed, all was good. Looking back, my feeling of being overlooked was only temporarily resolved through helping people. I filled the voids around those times of helping with food. In particular, I sought foods high in sugar, refined carbohydrates and fats. The crime had been committed and I had been given my life sentence.

Given a life sentence

Notice that I said, 'I had been given my life sentence'. This is a very important distinction because, being given this life sentence has an inference of a gift rather than simply pulling a Chance card as you would in Monopoly. I believe there is a greater design and purpose in the weaknesses and challenges that seem to randomly manifest through our formative years.

I suggest that we are not simply programmed passengers. We have been involved in the decision to take on these filters. Our life sentence… 'hath had elsewhere its setting, and cometh from afar: Not in entire forgetfulness, and not in utter nakedness, but trailing clouds do we come from God, who is our home'. I share Wordsworth's jail metaphor when he went on to write, 'Heaven lies about us in our infancy! Shades of the jail house begin to close upon the growing boy…' He even referred to the grown man as the 'Inmate Man'.

Childhood is not defined by the age of a person. By that I mean, when we are still imprisoned by our life sentence, we are still speaking, understanding and thinking with the filters of the child. We could be old and on death's door and still be functioning from this childhood narrative. In my case that would mean I would still be looking to be

The unintentional crime

validated though my ability to help people. If there wasn't a way I could be of help, I would resort to comfort eating and other addictive behaviours to fill the empty emotional space.

This is why dieting is generally unsuccessful. When the child is dominant in your psyche as an adult, and food has served as your pacifier, dieting causes serious problems in those times when you are fully identifying with your story of poor self-worth. When you resort to food, eating is your lifebuoy and without it you have to tread water. Dieting is treading water and you work hard at staying afloat. All the while the seven-year-old keeps reminding you of your failings and inadequacies.

Eventually you reach a breaking point, and the effort to keep dieting, or treading water, is too much. You reach out for your lifebuoy and resort to comfort eating. The shame of failure reinforces your story of poor worth, which ups the ante on your comfort eating. You end up putting on more weight rather than losing it.

The only way to effectively lose weight is to recognise your true worth, which is to be free of your story, and become aligned with a more self-honouring lifestyle. Then, the way you relate to food is a natural expression of the love you have for yourself.

Get Out of Jail Card

To become the aware adult, we have to put away childish things, which in this context is our story. The natural consequence of relinquishing our life sentence is that we are pardoned from our jail. Once we are released from jail we get to live life as an aware adult. Only then do we establish a sense of our real worth. In order to relinquish our life sentence, we have to first know what it is. We can't change what we aren't aware of.

chapter 2

Your life sentence

So, what is a life sentence? It is a one-line sentence, an executive summary of sorts, that summarises your story. The story is a personally held belief of poor self-worth that moulds the bricks that form the walls of your prison. In my case, those bricks were depression, obesity, divorce and bankruptcy, but more about that later. The bricks are laid with mortar made up of your core fear and self-doubt.

To better understand this, I will illustrate what I mean through my own story. In the last chapter you heard the details of my formative years. Effectively, that is my story, and what emerged was my life sentence.

The life sentence that emerged for me was 'In order to know that I matter, I need to be noticed.' Anyone who knows me, and who is reading this will be laughing out loud and nodding their heads knowing how true that is. I felt that, if I found a stage or could do something to help people, I would be noticed. My idea was, that if I could get noticed, then I must be OK.

Building your own jail

My earliest recollection of natural healing was in the early 60's when I was about six, accompanying my grandmother to her regular remedial massage sessions. I

Your life sentence

can clearly recall the smell of camphor. I was intrigued by the tapotement, as I couldn't imagine how someone would voluntarily want to be slapped. What I do recollect was how happy Grandma was after the massage, and Grandma wasn't always that happy. I accompanied my mother several years later to the Osteopath, and saw the same benefits being enjoyed by her.

I rationalised that if I could help people feel this good, they would like me and I would be noticed. That would make everything better. I talked to my parents about the possibility of studying Remedial Massage or Osteopathy and saw the immediate pleasure that this idea brought my mother. I had finally found a way to be noticed by my mother.

In my last two years of high school, I was offered an opportunity to work with an Osteopath during the school holidays. His validation of my natural ability further fuelled my interest in studying natural therapies. My dad built a massage table and, at 15, I began to do massages for family and friends. Word spread and my little after school business grew. You can imagine how delighted I was being noticed in this way.

By the time I reached my late teens, I had fully identified with my story and my life sentence, albeit unconsciously. So much so, I made the decision to pursue a career in natural health because I could see the kudos attributed to other health practitioners for the difference they had made in others' lives. I wanted to be noticed and appreciated in a similar way. Not being aware of the motive, I decided it would be a good idea to make natural health my career.

Research into my career path revealed the need to study in Sydney. The college was 1000 kilometres from home. I had just turned 17, and I would be leaving all of my friends (who went to Brisbane to go to university) as well as my family. I would be going to a place that was unfamiliar and where I would mostly be alone. Although I considered my options, the chance of finding my treasure, the thing that I valued most, totally displaced any concerns. I was off to Sydney.

The rest of my life has been impacted by this decision, which as you recall was inspired by my life sentence. The child and his needs were pulling my strings, of which I was totally oblivious.

Take a moment to consider your own story and how it influenced the choices you made through your formative years. How did those choices impact on the rest of your life? Over the years of mentoring I have helped many people identify their life sentences. I've listed a few below:

Your life sentence

- No matter how hard I try, I'll never be good enough.
- I am never supported in what I want to do.
- No matter what I do, the world will reject me at any turn.
- I'm different and I don't belong.
- Through high achievement, I'll get noticed.
- I only matter when validated by the opposite sex.
- In order to avoid feeling unimportant, I must work hard at being desirable and of value.
- To be me and to be safe, I have to live in my own shell.
- I have to be in control to survive.

The reason that I call these one-liners a life sentence is because they result in us living inside a jail of attitudes, beliefs and expectations that never change. Our jail is the life we live constrained by that story. Everything about our life experience is created from that one sentence.

What do you value?

We each have at our disposal resources that we can 'spend' however we choose. Time is the one resource that is a constant for us all. There are always only 24 hours in a day. Sure, some people live longer than others, but through the course of a day we all have the same amount of time at our disposal.

Talent is another resource and represents the application of ability. Some people have more talent than others, but it's more important how much we use the talent we possess. Money and possessions, like talent, varies from person to person but, as with talent, we can do a lot with little, or a little with a lot. How we choose to 'spend' or use our resources indicates what we value and treasure most.

Having spent years talking to people about values, I came to the realisation that very few people are consciously aware of what they value. That's really unfortunate given that values are to a human what a rudder and keel are to a boat. The directional vision or purpose that someone holds, represents the source of power that propels the boat. Values give stability and a greater capacity to maintain a true course, especially in times of turbulence.

The best way to identify what you value most is to answer the following two questions:

On what do I spend my resources?

What do I expect to get by spending my resources in that way?

Regarding the first question, the majority of people will indicate that the most significant use of their time is their

Your life sentence

job. It's the next question that reveals all. It answers the question 'why'. You might work to earn the wages that support your lifestyle. You might put in lots of overtime to avoid spending time at home. You might work to fulfil a need to be of authentic service to humanity. You might work because you love what you do.

You see, why you work makes a difference. I have observed that whatever you expect to get from working is a strong indicator of what you value. And the thing that you value is a significant clue for understanding the nature of your life sentence.

Collecting the evidence

Consider for a moment how you spend your money. The two big areas of financial commitment are housing and food. On the surface that seems reasonable, but let's look at why you spend the money on housing in the way that you do. You might be renting or you could be purchasing a home. The type of home you buy or rent, and even why you would do one or the other, reflects your values.

Owning a home might give you security. Renting a house allows freedom. You might feel you need to have a house that impresses, with lots of mod cons. You might have a minimalist philosophy and choose to live in a simple home, uncluttered and with few possessions. It could also be that your minimalist approach justifies your lack of abundance and makes your scarcity consciousness acceptable.

Where you live could be for status, practicality or just because you like the environment. You might be living in the same town or even the same street as where you grew up. This might placate your fear of change or fear of disappointing your parents. You might be living somewhere as far away from family as you can get. You could be escaping skeletons, or want to express yourself without being judged by people you know. Where you live, and why, is evidence of what you value. And what you value arises out of your life sentence.

Everything about our life experience is created from our story. Even the people we marry end up being inspired by our story and generally turn out to be clones of our parents, who are central to our story. It is like we have been programmed to marry our mum or dad. Some of us are too smart for that, and rebel by marrying the total opposite of our parent. Either way, our choice is being informed by our story — just different sides of the same coin.

It gets even more weird. People divorce and, not having resolved their life sentence, find themselves right back in another relationship, which in essence mimics the one they just left. Consider a woman who leaves one abusive relationship only to find herself in another one much the same. Typically, she was raised in a home where this type of abuse was modelled. She developed a filter that blocks out the ability to recognise a loving man. Even if he appears, he is invisible to her. Her poor self-worth filters him out. She only sees the ones who match what she perceives she was worth.

When something is observed it changes

Of course, there is another way of engaging life, without our story and our life sentence. We can do this by developing new values that inform how we live life.

New values would mean that we would choose to spend our time, talent and money in different ways. In fact, the impact of adopting new values can be so far reaching I have seen people change jobs, move house, and leave relationships — effectively totally transforming their lives. The radical nature of these changes become one of the biggest obstacles people face as they become more aware of their story.

When something can be observed with true awareness it

transforms, it changes. This is one of the supporting principles to change. It suggests that all that is required for change to occur is authentic awareness. So, I will give you a warning right now. If you continue to read this book and continue to become more aware of your life sentence and the way in which it does not serve you, then you are in danger of encountering radical change in your life.

Are you ready for that?

This state of observation is in fact the state of mindfulness, which is the catalyst for change. Mindfulness is remembering in each instant that you have a choice, a choice between your habitual way of living life, which is responsible for a reality you want to avoid, or a more self-honouring reality that brings you the life you love. Through a pragmatic approach to enhancing your awareness you can create both the more self-loving alternative for your life, and the strategies needed to create it.

The emerging concept of neuroplasticity is fundamental to the theory that being more aware, and being mindful of that awareness, can foster sustainable change. Every time you consider a more serving or self-loving alternative you feed the development of a new neural pathway. This is the foundation to a new habit, a more serving habit. With repeated mindfulness, the newly formed self-loving

Your life sentence

alternative builds to the point where it becomes the neural path of least resistance. At that stage, you naturally choose the more self-loving behaviours. With what is called neural pruning, the old neural pathway of axons and dendrites disassembles and the old habits disappear.

Working out your life sentence

Go and find a notebook and pen and allow yourself as much time as is necessary to work though the following process:

1. What causes you to be extremely happy? Why?

2. What causes you to be very unhappy? Why?

3. What do you fear that fuels both your happiness and unhappiness?

4. What have you done throughout your life to dodge that fear? (List several)

5. What is the reoccurring theme to your answers in 4?

6. Regarding your approach to life, are you more motivated to seek the things that make you extremely happy, or avoid the things that tend to make you very unhappy?

7. If you are more motivated to seek happy things, what is it that you want most?

8. If you are motivated to avoid unhappy things, what is it that you want to avoid the most?

9. Complete the following sentence with your answer to 7 or 8, depending on which one you were most aligned with.

    In order to (get/avoid)...

10. Complete the following with a summary of your answer in 5.

    I...

11. The combination of 9 and 10 is your story. Write your story out in one sentence below.

You might recall that my life sentence read this way. In order to matter, I need to be noticed.

Your life sentence (story)

It almost seems too trivial that you could boil it down to one sentence. Take a moment to reflect on that sentence and contemplate its significance on how you live your

Your life sentence

life today. How has it played out in your relationships, your career choice, your self-esteem, your health and wellbeing? Typically, you are not aware of the life sentence because it plays out sub-consciously. This life sentence has been fundamental to the formation of your life experience but it has also imprisoned you, compelling you to live your life through your fear. That fear is what has kept you in your personal jail. Whatever tool you use to sustainably release you from that fear is your 'Get Out of Jail' card.

Get Out of Jail Card

"When we are imprisoned by our story we are still speaking, understanding and thinking as a child."

Russell Sturgess

chapter 3

Life in jail

I need to be noticed

Having an audience, and helping others, was the way I got noticed. In my mind, if I was noticed it meant I was liked and or loved, which in turn meant I must have some worth. You will observe that everything about my worth was qualified by how I imagined others related to me. As I understood the evolution of this process, I realised the need that I perceived, which became what I valued, arose from the circumstances of my infancy.

Through the trial and error of my childhood, I developed attitudes, beliefs and behaviours that, as effectively as possible, strove to meet that need. When I got to adolescence, I then had to work out a way those 'get-my-needs-met strategies' could relate to the adult world. So, I worked out that helping people through healing would get me what I wanted and consequently chose a career path which provided that opportunity.

During my adolescence I discovered that I would be

noticed if I was in front of an audience. So, for four out of the five years I was in high school, I had one of the lead roles in the school play; I participated in the local theatre group; got involved in school debating; and took every opportunity to do public speaking. I recently came across one of my senior yearbooks which included a quote about my debating prowess by the Head of the English Department who said, 'Sturgess was magnificent!' I was noticed. (By the way, it's the only high school year book that I have kept!)

As if having an audience wasn't enough, I also sought validation through being involved in youth service activities. I participated in Interact (the high school version of Rotary); joined the Christian Youth Group and Junior Arts Council, along with service projects sponsored by my church; and participated in Scouts and the local community. I also volunteered two hours a week to help rehabilitate a young boy who had brain damage.

As you can imagine, participating in all of these extra-curricular activities meant that I didn't place a lot of focus on my academic pursuits. My life sentence was already beginning to engineer the structure of my jail. I didn't fail high school — in fact I managed to be on the high side of average, but it wasn't important to me. Remember, intelligence had already been claimed by my older brother.

Get Out of Jail Card

I didn't have an academic strategy for getting my needs met like my brother, mine was an emotional strategy.

At one stage, I recall expressing my interest in pursuing a career in performing arts. Unfortunately, my father was narrow-minded enough to believe that you couldn't make a living through the arts, and that most of the 'arty' people were 'poofters'. My interest in natural medicine was made more palatable by the fact that our family had been visiting Chiropractors and Osteopaths since the late sixties, so it ticked all of the boxes that I perceived would help me to get my infant needs met.

Building the jail

By the age of 17, I had established how I could move forward in the adult world and be noticed while being a helper. The foundations of my jail had been firmly laid. I went to college to study Osteopathy and Remedial Massage Therapy, and so the walls of my jail began to take form.

I drove to college in my 1948 Morris Z, painted Barbados Green. I was stylish in my dress and reasonably easy on the eye (people said I looked like Donny Osmond or Mark Holden). So I lapped up the attention. On reflection, I have often thought that these were some of the best years of my life — my jail was only partly built and the gaps in the wall still let in the Divine light that comes 'from God, who is our home'.

Of this time Wordsworth wrote, 'But he (the Boy) beholds the light, and when it flows, he sees it in his joy; The youth, who daily farther from the east must travel, still is Nature's Priest. Any by the vision splendid is on his way attended'.

He meant that in spite of the 'shades of the jail house' beginning to grow, the boy, and the youth, are still in touch with the Divine. But Wordsworth continued, 'At length the Man perceives it die away, and fade into the light of common day.' By the time the jail walls are finally complete, which can take a lifetime, the inmate is cut off from Divine light.

At age 18, I deferred my studies for two years to embrace another part of my life sentence. I became a proselytising missionary for the church I belonged to. I felt noticed within my church community and it fed my sense of worth through being able to 'save' people.

On my return, I completed my studies and met my future wife. She was a stunning part-time model. I revelled in her reflected beauty because it helped me to get noticed. In my naivety, I was under the belief that I was marrying for love, but there was more to it than that. My father's criteria for choosing a wife was that she should be able to cook, sew and play the piano. Dad must have repeated that mantra 100 times, if not more throughout my formative years. His mother met that criteria, his wife met that criteria, and my now my fiancé also ticked that box.

My mum was raised in a home where love was not expressed orally or physically. She experienced very few hugs or nurturing touch. As such, she only expressed love in the way she knew, by fulfilling her role as a mother and homemaker. Only recently has she spoken the words, 'I love you'. Subconsciously, I perceive that my choice of wife would result in the love I sought from my mother, in a way that had been limited in my infancy. The need to be noticed by being loved and nurtured by my mother, compounded my story and added more bricks to the jail wall.

Securing the jail

I went on to develop one of the busiest and successful practices in Remedial Massage Therapy, in my state. By the age of 35, I was treating over 120 clients a week, I had three children, I had built a beautiful home, I was driving a sports car and life appeared to be sweet. But don't be fooled, because life in jail is never that good.

Life in jail

The three strategies of my adolescence that I had unconsciously determined would help me to get noticed, were still serving me — helping people though my work as a healer; involvement in community service; and being on stage. I had a hugely successful practice and people told me on a regular basis how helpful I was. I was Group Leader of the local Scout group; I was involved in the school Parents & Citizens Association; I was a lay-minister in my church and involved in the local basketball association; I was showered with accolades from people regarding my community contribution. My adolescent strategy was working well.

My life sentence still held me in my jail. The primary evidence that things weren't right? I weighed over 140 kilograms.

Typically, the older we get, the higher the bar is raised in terms of the way we engage our strategies. I wasn't content unless I found a bigger stage. Through a series of synergistic occurrences, I was offered an opportunity to talk at conferences and conventions in the USA. This lead to me running a series of workshops through the USA, New Zealand and Australia. I could be away teaching for weeks on end, and did this for years. I was appointed as State Deputy Chief Commissioner in Scouting, and was part of the medical team for the NBL Brisbane Bullets. I was also highly positioned within my religion. I was being noticed nationally, internationally and spiritually. My adolescent strategies were working on a grand scale. The more sophisticated my dedication, the more complete my jail became.

But a day came in my clinic where I lost the desire to continue my work as a healer. I quickly sold my practice and walked away. I had over five thousand clients and was making a very comfortable living. It took me years to work out why, but I had reached a point where the drug that satisfied my need to be noticed required more than the 125 people a week I was helping.

When you don't understand your own worth (driven by the story of your child-self), you never believe it when you hear it from others, no matter how many people tell you. Having 125 people a week telling me I was great still wasn't enough. I needed the 126th person, and by this point there was no more time in my week to squeeze in client 126. Given how big my stage had become, I didn't need the clinic anymore in order to be noticed. I had found a bigger and better way to be seen. Now I know that all of this was being driven by a seven-year-old, who was wanting to be noticed, who was wanting to be valued. The treadmill I had created was subconsciously in response to my infant self.

The jail keeper

Because choices for engaging life were based on my life sentence, it makes sense that they were unsustainable. It didn't matter how many people told me what a gifted healer I was and how much I had helped, I couldn't hear them. It didn't matter how many people told me what a great teacher I was and how their lives has been touched. It didn't matter how many people expressed gratitude for all that I had done in my various roles in community service. It wasn't that I didn't believe them, I just couldn't hear them. I was too absorbed in listening to the voice of the insatiable seven-year-old. My jail-keeper was me as a seven-year-old.

The truth revealed

The problem with our life sentence is that, in our search for the ultimate treasure, which is the unshakeable belief that we are loveable just the way we are, we have learnt to hear only one voice — the child. Eventually our ignorance brings us to an impasse as our unsustainable choices reveal their true colours. With the passage of time, I lost my passion for healing, because the rewards lost their potency, like a drug requiring ever bigger doses.

Eventually I lost my passion for the staged presentations because, like the clinic, the energy I gained from it lost its potency. I constantly needed larger classes. I had a limit to the amount of energy I could muster to produce the courses and material, promote and arrange the workshops and live out of a suitcase for weeks on end.

Burnout and depression are the consequences of trying to satisfy the demands of your life sentence. Once burnout or depression happens, a domino effect follows and all other unsustainable behaviours unravel. My service opportunities became difficult to maintain. I had promised the earth and all I was able to give in the end was dirt.

My marriage came unstuck when my wife, could no longer fill the role of my surrogate mother (although at that time I would not have used that term). I was beginning to struggle financially, we had to sell our home, and I had an affair. It was only a matter of time before we separated and divorced.

Damage to others

I was still only listening to the needs of the child who was wanting to be noticed, most particularly by his mother. I found myself having a series of relationships with women who I unconsciously perceived would fulfil the need of the seven-year-old me, to be nurtured. It didn't matter how many women offered me that love, I was too absorbed in listening to the story of the seven-year-old who always needed more attention.

My actions were a catalyst which hurt some wonderful women, for which I am truly remorseful. If I had been more aware, if I had been free of my story and out of my jail, I would have truly seen them. Regretfully, all I heard were the demands of my inner-child. My jail led to several damaged relationships, which is typical of these types of sentences.

My relationship with my children was also impacted by my life sentence. Weeks and months of absence while I travelled internationally; hours preoccupied with work and community service; and too many moments of unjustified anger bought on by my own pain. Ironically, I was becoming the preoccupied parent of my own childhood, the very cause of my own life sentence.

Get Out of Jail Card

Referring to his own parental shortcomings my dad often said, 'A man should be horse-whipped'. Of course, this would not be appropriate in any circumstance but it indicated his deep regret. It didn't matter how much my children sought my attention, travelling and being on stage meant I would be noticed much more than just by being a dad. I see the impact of that in the lives of my, now adult, children for which I am deeply saddened.

No stillness in jail

You know that you are in jail when your life is without inner stillness. Stress, anger, jealousy, elation, grief, fear, being 'in love', anticipation and regret are some of the emotions of life that take us out of that inner stillness. Then there is our life sentence. As I reflect on my time in jail, I realise there was no inner stillness. I had moments of stillness as a child and as an adolescent, but by my 18th birthday it had gone. Explaining the nature of this jail Wordsworth wrote, 'Earth fills her laps with pleasures of her own…the homely Nurse doth all she can to make her foster-child, her Inmate Man, forget the glories he hath known and that imperial palace whence he came.'

chapter 4

Getting out of jail

Get Out of Jail Card

I remember when I turned 18, not long after I went to Sydney to study natural therapies, I had what I would call a nervous breakdown. The challenge of being away from home, on my own in a city the size of Sydney, having lived in a small country town up until that time, became too much for me to handle. I walked into my bedroom one afternoon after work, and broke down sobbing. I collapsed onto my bed. I still remember this as if it happened yesterday.

In those days there weren't mobile phones, Skype or Facebook. My parents would generally write to me every two weeks. Phone calls were mostly restricted to emergencies and birthdays and, even then, from my end of things, it would be reverse-charge from a public phone.

I had been raised in a religious home and had a fundamental Christian faith in God. I recall that while I was sobbing, I resorted to prayer for the first time in years. I said something like, "God, if you exist, help me!"

What happened next left an indelible memory. I heard a voice (a voice I now call the Still Small Voice) which said, "Russell, peace, be still. Everything is all right, you are held in my love." At the time, I thought what I heard was a voice, but later I realised that I had heard it in the centre of my being and not with my ears. As the words were spoken I immediately felt the most amazing sense of stillness and

Getting out of jail

overwhelming love — certainly enough to displace my fear. I had been gifted a moment of grace, a moment of stillness, which in that instant filled me with confidence and relief.

Wordsworth explained it this way, "The Youth, who daily father from the east must travel, is still Nature's priest, and by the vision splendid, is on his way attended."

Attempting to escape

Over the years, I tried on many occasions to escape the pressures which arose from being in jail. I went on many diets and successfully lost weight, only to put it back on (plus some). I gave up clinical practice and replaced it with teaching and public speaking, and still sought comfort through food and surrogate mothers. I even went on to give up teaching and public speaking because I could see they, like my clinical practice, were impacting on my health and wellbeing.

Having relinquished those attention seeking avenues, I unconsciously found a new one. I tried my hand at being noticed and valued through an academic approach. I wrote and self-published an academic book. This escape was equivalent to digging a tunnel under the jail. It took me three years full-time to build this escape route, only to find myself ending back in jail, resulting in depression and financial complications. In those three years, I used all of my financial resource to support and sustain me. By the time I published the book, I was broke.

Food in jail

I observed that when I was healing or doing community service I used savoury food to fill the empty spaces, and when I was on the stage, I would crave sweet food. After my three years book writing and publishing, followed by a couple of years of depression, I thought whatever was bothering me was out of my system. I thought I would be able to move forward in a way that would not compromise my health and wellbeing.

When an opportunity arose to teach one of my old courses, I was naive to think I had been away from the stage long enough to be able to do it without issues reappearing. The workshop went really well so, on the Sunday night after we finished class, I decided I wanted to go and get something to eat. Totally unaware of the unrelenting nature of my life sentence, I got frustrated when I couldn't find anywhere open to buy a sweet treat. I became very angry and unreasonable and, as one is prone to do, projected my anger onto my partner. We went to bed not talking.

Getting out of jail

Next morning, I awoke with clarity about what had happened the night before. I realised I was still stuck in my old patterns of behaviour, although I had still not identified my life sentence. The break from teaching had not been long enough — I hadn't been released from my jail. I didn't take to the stage for another 12 months.

A year later I was invited to talk about my newly published book at a conference. At the conference I received very flattering compliments about my work by people I admired. I had really been noticed! I had dinner at the conference and travelled home with a sense of satisfaction. I had been driving less than 30 minutes before the thought popped into my head that I could pull into the next service station and get an ice cream. As the thought crossed my mind, I immediately realised the behaviours that were compromising my health were still active in my consciousness. I felt like I was never going to be able to get over my eating habit — I still didn't understand how my experience was being governed by my life sentence.

Dead man walking

In 2010 I was depressed and on the verge of bankruptcy. I had been in solitary confinement with my depression and was about to do hard labour with my impending bankruptcy. I was locked in my self-imposed imprisonment without even knowing it. The irony was, I had written a book that revealed an ancient formula for finding inner stillness. It explained how one got into jail, and how to get out of it. As much as I had the knowledge, I didn't have the self-understanding. While coming to terms with the fact that my book wasn't a Chance card to fame and fortune, I was inspired to develop my awareness mentoring program.

I decided I needed to personally trial the program. I completed profiling of my own mental, physical, emotional and spiritual awareness, and it was plainly obvious that there were noticeable deficiencies. My physical awareness first and foremost was well below par, and if I was going to do anything with this program, I had to walk my talk. I was obese and unfit. I had to bring my health into balance.

When using the EAP awareness profiling tool, I was surprised to learn that my spiritual awareness could only be described, at best, as being 'somewhat aware'. My personal perception was that spiritually, I was 'mostly aware'. There was a gap between perception and reality. It should have been plainly obvious that if I was suffering as much as I was at that time, (divorce, bankruptcy, obesity and depression), something was seriously incongruent spiritually.

While researching my book, I came across a reference to the Camino de Santiago, a medieval pilgrimage trail traversing northern Spain. At the time of my research, it left no impression but, as I was working out how to resolve my lack of physical and spiritual awareness, a chance conversation with a friend about the Camino triggered a compulsion to walk it. I took 15 months to prepare. In that time, I lost 25 kilograms, while walking up to 100 kilometres a week.

In September 2011, I began a walk of 40 days and nights covering a distance of just over 1000 kilometres. It was a physical pilgrimage, but it was also spiritual. Because I had resolved so much of my physical imbalance prior to walking the Camino, the walk became more about who I was spiritually.

The walk helped me identify how my spirituality was out of balance and that my values needed readjustment. I began to scratch the surface and understand the association between my suffering, my life sentence, and my values — and ultimately, my self-worth.

The Camino

On the Camino, I walked for 30 days averaging just over 30 kilometres a day, taking the occasional tourist break in the larger cities. I mostly walked by myself, although I met people from all over the world each day. Most days I walked for six or seven hours, giving me plenty of opportunity to reflect on my life and how it ended up being such a mess. I recognised a pattern and, at its foundation, was poor self-esteem.

I began to get an inkling of my story, but it remained elusive. As I walked, I had a mantra that I repeated many times each day. I even managed to learn it in Spanish! It became an anchor for my mind. It's amazing how easily the mind can wander when the feet are wandering.

> 'Padre nuestro, que esta's en el cielo,
> Santificado sea tu nombre.
> Venga a nosotros tu reino:
> Hagase tu voluntad en la tierra como en el cielo.
> Danos hoy nuestro pan de cada día.
> Perdona nuestras ofensas,
> como también nosotros perdonamos a los que nos ofenden.
> No nos dejes caer en tentación y libranos del mal.
> Amen.
> (The Lord's Prayer)

Through days of contemplation, I began to realise that throughout my life I had only related to my world (unconsciously) in the context of my ego and my need to be the centre of attention. I hadn't made the link that

Getting out of jail

the emotional needs of my child-self were continually controlling the way I, as an adult, engaged my life. I stayed in the awareness of my ego agenda for days, and then about two-thirds of the way across the Camino I had an experience that transformed my life. It affected how the rest of my life would unfold from that point forward.

Release from jail

It was a weekend in late October. I had exchanged my pilgrim hat for my tourist hat, spending two days in the beautiful northern Spanish city of Leon. I had just finished crossing the Meseta, a flat desolate plain covering a distance of about 250 kilometres between Burgos and Astorga. Some pilgrims who walk the Camino skip this part by catching a bus. The endless flat terrain and monotonous scenery means that you get to spend copious amounts of time in your head, and that was just what I needed.

I was resting in a city that was truly an oasis following an arduous week of walking. On the Sunday, I met other pilgrims at a bar in the Plaza de San Martin over lunch. As I only had a few photos of myself on the Camino I asked them to take some pictures of me with my camera. With engaging conversation, the pictures were soon forgotten.

Get Out of Jail Card

On my first night in Leon, I stayed at the Benedictine albergue, San Maria de Carbajal. A pilgrim benediction was held by the nuns at 9.30pm. Back in the albergue shortly afterwards, lights were out by 10.30pm. As with previous curfews, if I wasn't ready to sleep I would lay on my darkened bunk bed and review the photos I had taken through the day. I kept the ones I liked and deleted the ones I didn't.

As I reviewed the pictures from that day, I looked at the photo taken at lunch. What I saw was someone who was truly happy. Someone who naturally expressed stillness and who obviously possessed a great sense of their worth. Instantly I burst into tears and muffled my sobs of joy as I was filled with an almost indescribable love for myself. I'm

Getting out of jail

not sure why I stifled my response, since I was sharing a room with 50 other pilgrims, half of whom were snoring.

The feeling of peace and love was exactly the same as what I had experienced 35 years previously when, at 18 years old while attending college in Sydney. As the tears flowed freely I suspected at that moment I was seeing myself as God sees me.

In that instant, the child's story that had become my life sentence was redundant. I had finally been noticed by the one person who needed to notice me most — me! In that one instant, that twinkling of an eye, I was unconsciously paroled from my life sentence. I no longer needed a stage for people to notice me. I no longer needed to be a healer or overcommit to doing community service in order to be noticed and to establish my worth. I no longer needed my mother to notice me or love me anymore. I was able to see myself and love myself as I imagine God loves me. I had been set free.

Two days after I left Leon I walked 53 kilometres in one day, which included crossing the 1,500 metre pass over Monte Irago, the highest point of the Camino. Such was my energy level and sense of freedom, I could have kept walking, but darkness put an end to that notion. I finally understood the Irish blessing, 'May the road rise to meet you and the wind always be at your back'.

The 'Get Out of Jail' card

The only true 'Get Out of Jail' card is the voice you hear that replaces the lifelong chatter of your child-self. There are two voices capable of voiding that sound. One is the aware-adult-voice. This is the internal voice that can rationally identify all the healthy aspects of your consciousness. It contradicts what your child-self has had to say about you throughout your life. There is also the Still Small Voice, the voice of the Divine that only speaks of love and stillness. In any instant, you can choose to which of the two new voices you will pay attention.

Once you are aware of your jail, the only way that you return to it is by ignoring the aware-adult-voice or the Still Small Voice, giving your attention to the demands of your child voice. It's not easy to ignore the child voice. It has been your master and, like sheep with their shepherd, it's the only voice you have responded to your whole life. To respond to

Getting out of jail

a new shepherd takes time and practice, placing you in a tenuous position that in jail language is called your 'period of parole'. Be careful not to breach your parole, as you will find yourself back in jail.

It has been my observation that significant changes in consciousness (for better or worse) take two years before manifesting in form. I first observed this with people who developed chronic diseases like cancer. Often, they had experienced a major life trauma, with associated emotional suffering, that predated their disease symptoms by approximately two years. Anecdotally, this alluded to the notion that changes in consciousness facilitates changes in physical wellbeing.

If significant imbalances in consciousness result in disease, then it can be assumed that creating a balanced consciousness may result in health and wellbeing. It could also be expected that the time it takes to manifest disease might be indicative of the time it takes to manifest healing. This infers that it will take about two years of commitment to stop listening to the child's voice and become attuned to the aware-adult-voice and/or the Still Small Voice. Much has been written about people who have resolved chronic disease by changing their state of consciousness To learn more, I suggest Dr Dean Ornish's book Love and Survival.

A symbol of consciousness

This theory and observation is based on the idea that our body is a symbol of consciousness. By that I mean, when we experience a significant change in our thinking; in our emotions; the way we relate to our senses; or in what we desire as reflected in our values — changes take place in the tissues of the body. This then changes the way the body functions.

In my Remedial Therapy program, Fascial Kinetics, this concept is explained in detail. Thinking is associated with dryness in the body. Feelings relate to wetness. Sensing relates to coldness. Desiring relates to heat.

Any suffering that brings change to the states of hot, dry wet, and cold in the human body, when sustained over long periods, results in disease. Of course, the suffering can be a direct result of our life sentence. A restoration of the balance to those elements, when sustained over long periods, results in healing. Positive results require a release from the life sentence through a life lived in awareness and mindfulness.

For many years prior to walking the Camino, I had suffered from severely cracked heels. I tried a lot of topical applications, some of which gave relief for short periods of time. I tried changes in diet and prescribed nutritional supplements, but to no lasting benefit. This was a hereditary problem as I shared it with my siblings. Cracked heels are caused by a state of dehydration and possibly compromised circulation. As indicated above, dryness is associated with one's state of thinking. Those who know me and my siblings understand that thinking is an important part of how we turn up in the world.

An interesting thing happened on my return from the Camino. Almost seven years on and I have only had one cracked heel. Sure my heels can be dry, but they don't crack and debilitate me with pain like they used to. I have observed that when I get into extended periods of mental concentration, my heels get dryer but they still don't crack. The Camino was significant for me in that it was a journey from my head into my heart. Not only has that resulted in a softening of my attitude and approach to life, it has also resulted in a softening of the tissues of my body.

Get Out of Jail Card

"Awareness is gaining the understanding, mindfulness is holding the understanding in life."

Russell Sturgess

chapter 5

Out on parole

Get Out of Jail Card

On the Camino, I had many opportunities to experience inner stillness. This was more the case during the last four days, when I stayed in Finisterre, at the end of my pilgrimage. This seaside fishing village was to become significant in my life's journey.

For some years prior to walking the Camino, I had been collecting miniature fishing boats crafted from wood, all about 15 centimetres in length. In total I had nine, red, white, green and blue boats. They sat head-height on a shelf just above my work desk where I saw them almost every day. My fascination in collecting the boats started after a vivid dream. When I awoke, I had a clear vision of a fishing village that I felt would be significant in my life journey. The impression the dream left was so deep, I was able to recall every detail and was inspired to start collecting these boats to help keep the dream alive. For years my grandson had wanted to play with them but I denied his requests. Ironically, just a few months before I walked the Camino, I decided that this dream/omen held no more significance and gave all of the boats to my grandson — much to his delight.

It was my last day of walking the Camino and I was just a couple of kilometres from my final destination. As I rounded the bay towards the cape, I saw before me the fishing village I had seen in my dream all those years before.

Out on parole

There were the red, green, white and blue fishing boats bobbing on the water, corralled in the harbour. The scene was set against a backdrop of shops and houses and a small cliff separated the high street and the main part of the village from the harbour, just as I remembered. Once again, I had cause for tears as I made my way towards the boats. I didn't know what the significance was in the big picture, but I knew being here was important.

My calling

My Camino was intended to be a spiritual pilgrimage. The experience in Leon had been incredibly profound, since it was there that I got to be noticed — by me! Still without complete understanding about my life sentence, I knew what I had experienced in Leon was significant for my whole of life journey. This expanded awareness of my worth was what I was seeking when I decided to do the Camino.

My new awareness came with responsibility for how I turned up in the world. It became clear, during this time in Finisterre, that my new motive needed to be compassion — for myself and for others. I sensed that I would still be working with the mindfulness program I had developed but, instead of being motivated by my need to be noticed, I would be aligned with empathy, compassion and benevolence.

I had four days in Finisterre. Being off-season (the beginning of November), I was the only patron in my hostel, which meant there was little interruption to my state of peace. I had planned to leave Spain on my birthday, and strongly felt the need to perform a ritual before I went home that would symbolise the commitment I was prepared to make to this new focus. The day before my birthday, I still hadn't settled on a ritual, or who would officiate. I knew I wanted someone who possessed the necessary spiritual qualities to perform such a duty. I had met people along the Camino who were suitable for such a role, but none were in Finisterre.

On this, my last afternoon in Spain, I was in Plaza Santa Catalina using a public phone to call home, when the bus from Santiago pulled into the square. Two South African women who I had met on several occasions along the Camino disembarked. A couple of days walking together had given us the opportunity to spend several hours conversing, during which it became evident that we shared similar spiritual philosophies. One of the women, Terri, had done a lot of personal and spiritual development work. She and her friend were doing the Camino as a part of a spiritual discipline. Terri was someone I felt would be qualified to officiate in my ritual.

Later that evening I tracked them down and explained the vague concept of what I wanted to do. They enthusiastically agreed to meet me early the next day.

My last day in Spain

I awoke early on that last morning in Spain and sat bolt upright in bed. In that instant, I knew what my ceremony would be and what had to be said. Rather than the baptism I was considering (an immersion ritual on one of the beaches at the 'end of the world') it would be an anointing ritual, something akin to those practiced in the early Christian temples.

Get Out of Jail Card

I began to write as the words flooded into my mind. It took all of two minutes, I could barely write fast enough.

> I anoint your brow that your mind will be filled with peace, which will be foremost in your thoughts.
>
> I anoint your abdomen that the passion of your body will be turned to justice and assisting the needy.
>
> I anoint your right breast that your heart will remain open and full of mercy for all of mankind and for yourself.
>
> I anoint your left breast that your spirit will be filled with charity, the pure love of Christ, to be a light for others returning home.
>
> With this anointing you are invited to enter the Holy Place of the Temple of Your Soul, where all that you choose to be is guided by peace, justice, mercy and charity.
>
> Welcome into the House of God. From this day you will be a Son of God, no longer the son of man. Now you are called to do your Father's work. Relinquish your attachments to the world, and with humility and grace prepare to serve God, for this is the kingdom, the power and the glory, for ever and ever, amen.

Terri and Lynne met me in the plaza just after dawn on the morning of my 53rd birthday. We walked the three

Out on parole

kilometres to the Cape, dogged by light showers, but undeterred. There was a reverence to our demeanour as we all understood the sacred nature of this ceremony. Much of our conversation centred on our respective Camino adventures.

In my pack, I carried the ritual tools needed for the ceremony. They included a scallop shell that I found on the beach the day I completed my walk into Finisterre. Traditionally, pilgrims collected these as evidence that they had completed their penance. In some regard, my walk was my penance for my life sentence.

Oil was essential for such a ritual. With my understanding of these types of rituals I knew it needed to be consecrated (blessed for that specific purpose). Fortunately, earlier on in the Camino I had bought pure essential oil. So, before going to meet my friends I performed a prayer of consecration to dedicate it as anointing oil. This symbolically made it sacred oil.

With my scallop shell, consecrated oil and script in hand I went off to the designated meeting point. We found a suitable position nestled in amongst the large outcrop of rocks at the Cape. As if the ritual was being sanctioned, the showers stopped and the sun emerged for the first time that morning. Lynne served as the witness and Terri filled the role of officiate. The oil was poured into the scallop shell, which Lynne held. Then, while reading the script, Terri anointed four key points on my body with the oil.

I hadn't realised at the time, but I was freed from my jail. My dream about the boats and the harbour finally made sense. I wasn't fully cognitive of what really happened for two more years but, it signalled one of the most important times in my life.

Within hours I was on my way home, both literally and figuratively.

Being on parole

There is a commonly used eastern adage that goes, 'Before enlightenment, chop wood, carry water. After enlightenment, chop wood, carry water'. In other words nothing external changes, but everything internal changes. Being released from jail is the consequence of enlightenment. It's that moment when you know you are love, and consequently, you are divinely connected. Your story can't keep you in jail any longer. With this awareness

Out on parole

comes the necessity for establishing new values. The values that emerge from your life sentence have no place in your life anymore.

On leaving jail, your new found awareness means you experience inner peace more often. Your purpose and the values that will inform how you spend your time, talent and wealth will no longer be governed by your life sentence. They will now be divinely inspired. In your awareness, and the stillness that arises from that, you will voluntarily be prepared to say, 'Not my will, but your will be done'.

The parole period is a time needed to imagine and create a new expression for your life, aligned with your new desires and associated values. Following your epiphany, you return to chopping wood and carrying water. The difference now is that you no longer need what you did previously from your relationships, your work or your lifestyle.

In my case, I no longer required my partners to be my mother or admirers. I no longer sought the love outside of myself. I didn't have to be on a stage or be a healer/helper anymore. I was soundly aware of my intrinsic worth and nothing I did in my life could improve on that. I didn't have to live the way I had lived in the past. But old habits die hard.

Slipping back

About six months after I had returned home from the Camino, I went away for the weekend, with my partner of six years to spend some time with friends. On the Saturday night we went to a Spanish-styled tapas bar for dinner. I ordered Caldo Gallego soup, as it was one of my favourites while walking the Camino. The flavour was completely authentic and the taste immediately transported me back to my Camino in Spain. In the same instant, I was also reminded of the freedom and clarity gained on my pilgrimage, and the commitment I had made on my birthday on Cape Finisterre.

Out on parole

I was saddened and shocked with the realisation that a gap had emerged. I had lost touch with my inner peace. Tears filled my eyes as I realised that I had compromised my commitment to my purpose. I had all but forgotten the commitment I made on my birthday on that rocky outcrop at Finisterre.

Before the Camino, and subsequent to it, I had been struggling with my relationship. We had been sleeping separately for some time prior to the Camino, and the angst and stress of how we related was taking its toll. Without going into all of the details, I now know I was in this relationship because of my life sentence. I had chosen my partner because she was the antithesis of other unsuccessful partners. Unfortunately, the flip side of a coin, is still the same coin. I found myself in an intensifying prison of arguments, frustration, anger, passion and scarcity because of my life sentence. The love I sought from without, was even more elusive because I had strategically chosen a partner who could not fill my need for mother love. Let's just say I was too smart for my own good!

Back from the Camino, the need for seeking or avoiding love in a relationship had been replaced with the love I felt for myself and my commitment to my purpose. I was finally aware that I had worth. I no longer sought a sense of my value in a relationship as my experience in Leon made that mostly redundant. Yet, after six months of being on parole, I found myself slipping back to being under the influence of my life sentence — my childhood need to be noticed.

The Spanish soup woke me up. Returning home from that weekend away, I announced my need to be free of the ongoing stress of the relationship. I moved out to live on my own. I was really clear that stillness and inner peace were important to me and made two important decisions that supported that awareness. I wanted to live in a way that meant I could stay committed to my calling and I wanted to have sustainable inner peace in my life. Both of those seemed impossible while I remained in that relationship.

The separation was challenging. Yet again, my choices were impacting on someone else, and someone that I cared a lot about. I persevered and I got my life and my parole back on track. By re-engaging the awareness I gained on the Camino, and being clear about what I did and didn't want to experience, I tried to live a life guided by peace, justice, mercy and charity. In spite of all I had been through, I still hadn't consciously grasped that I had a life sentence and how it kept dragging me back into old patterns of behaviour.

In Buddhism it's taught that suffering is the result of three poisons — ignorance, avoidance and attachment. Jesus taught the same idea in the Parable of the Sower. In the Parable of the Sower, Jesus equates what happens to awareness with what happens to seeds when planted. In the first scenario, if the soil hasn't been worked, the seeds can't take root and being exposed, are either eaten by birds or die. This is Buddha's ignorance aspect — a sealed off mind.

Buddha's avoidance aspect relates to the seeds that fall into rocky ground. The seeds take root but can't get established, so the first bit of wind or bad weather knocks the seedlings over. In the third scenario, Buddha's attachment aspect, the seeds are planted in soil and grow into mature plants, but the unattended weeds overgrow the plants and choke them. This is like adopting new behaviours, which you can sustain for a time and then find yourself reverting to old habits. Sound familiar?

About relationships

Let's recap for a moment. As you may recall, I was looking for the mother-love in my relationships that I felt was absent in my childhood. Prior to meeting my then partner, I had unconsciously sought relationships with women who were strong 'mother archetypes' in order to find the love that I perceived I lacked from my childhood. This hole drove me in the same way that I needed to be on stage and to be a helper through charity work and healing. I was too absorbed in listening to the story of the seven-year-old who kept saying that he was still wanting to be noticed. Even if these relationships had the capacity to give me all of the love I needed, I just couldn't see it. I was blinded by my story.

At some stage, I had decided I needed someone who didn't meet the 'mother archetype' criteria. I knew I wasn't getting the love I wanted, and rationalised that finding someone who was 'not-a-mother' would solve the problem. She was my age, attractive, single, worked successfully in the corporate world and had no children. The perfect not-mother, the flip side of the mother-archetype coin. The capacity for this relationship to serve me was seen in my partner's ability to admire who I was and value my work in the world. I replaced the need for love with a need for admiration. It was just another form of being noticed.

During this time, I became aware of my 'need' to be noticed on a stage. Being more aware positively impacted my habitual eating habits around those occasions. I didn't display the same unconscious eating patterns associated with being noticed in that way. I had also become more aware around my 'need' to help, especially regarding my clinical work. Again, awareness caused my eating habits to change.

Out on parole

On my return from the Camino I was 56 kilograms lighter than my heaviest weight and a year on from the Camino, I had gained 15 kilograms. I had my head around my work, and my service triggers, and was satisfied that they were no longer contributing to my being overweight. I worked out that my greatest place of unhappiness was in my relationship and this had been contributing to my weight gain. The lack of joy and the ongoing arguments brought me a lot of stress. This was the one remaining place where poor food choices were being triggered. I unconsciously returned to my old survival strategy of eating comfort food.

I was still unaware of my story and how it was a part of what was going on. My choice to seperate was based purely on the observation of how my weight changes were linked to the relationship. I was still of the opinion that if I stopped the relationship, like I had stopped being a healer and stopped teaching, I would be OK. I do want to point out that what I am sharing is from my perspective. It doesn't necessarily reflect what was going on for my partner.

You can't change what you can't see

Within 18 months of our separation, my partner was back living in my 'peaceful' home almost full-time (although she hadn't officially moved in). I couldn't quite let go of the attachment Buddha talked about and the weeds Jesus described. If you do what you have always done you will get what you always got. Nothing changed, so the arguments and the associated stresses re-emerged. This was the parole period. On parole we are still being influenced by our life sentence.

As you can image, all through this time my weight was up and down like a yo-yo. Not only did I put on weight, but once again I lost momentum regarding the commitment made at the end of the Camino. I reflected on my 'soup awakening' 18 months previous and saw the same pattern re-emerge. I realised once again that things had to change. The fact that I kept repeating old patterns of behaviour I knew I had missed something important.

Around this time, I was mentoring a client when the whole idea of a life sentence came into existence. As she summarised her suffering, I heard myself observe, 'That's your life sentence'. Her whole life had been informed by a core self-belief, summed up in one sentence.

In that moment and in the days that followed, I began to identify my own life sentence and found the missing piece of my puzzle. I was now consciously aware that my life journey had been completely informed by one sentence — in order to matter, I needed to be noticed. I had held this belief since my childhood, and as such, became the voice to which I paid the most attention. Even with having had my Camino experience, of seeing myself as God sees me, I reverted to listening to the familiar voice of the seven-year-old me, the one who wanted to be noticed.

I realised that this was what kept me in this relationship. Up to that point, ignorance of the life sentence meant that creating a different relationship model would have been almost impossible. I shared with my on-again, off-again partner what I had discovered. She too was able to identify her story, and see how her life sentence had also imprisoned her. We had experienced enough pain in our relationship, that we were both desperate to be free of the impact of our respective life sentences. Finally, by becoming aware of our life sentences, it was possible to resolve our relationship, honouring both the love we each held for ourselves, and the love we had for each other.

We both made a commitment to stay aware of our respective life sentences, which had distracted us from our higher purpose. We also committed to living our lives in accordance with the highest expression of our individual values and vision. We separated once again, but this time fully aware of each other's story and respecting each other's desire to live in awareness and stillness.

Stillness

The parole period is extremely difficult, and I would suggest that once you know and understand your story, it can take two years, or more, before you get a full pardon. There are some simple markers that help keep you on the straight and narrow. Inner peace is the primary one. If you aren't experiencing inner peace, then you are in your life sentence. If you are choosing behaviours that aren't self-honouring — physically, mentally, emotionally and spiritually — then you are in your life sentence. Anytime you feel lonely, fearful, depressed, purposeless or stressed, you are in your life sentence. You will either live life in your life sentence or with inner peace. The one will eliminate the other, they cannot coexist.

This idea of living in with inner peace and stillness was beautifully expressed in a monologue found in Longfellow's play, The New England Tragedies. His Quaker character, Edith, is with several other Quakers who are about to be imprisoned and she gives this profound speech:

> 'Let us, then, labour for an inward stillness.
> An inward stillness and an inner healing;
> That perfect silence where the lips and the heart
> Are still, and we no longer entertain
> Our own imperfect thoughts and vain opinions.

Out on parole

> And God alone speaks in us, and we wait
> In singleness of heart, that we know
> His will, and in the silence of our spirits,
> That we may do his will, and do that only.'
> — Henry Wadsworth Longfellow

Longfellow makes it clear that when you come to that place of stillness you have singleness of heart. In other words, your heart is aligned with Divine Will, and your spirits, those things you desire, are silenced, since you will be committed to only doing the Will of God. In stillness you are in relationship with the Divine. As the Old Testament Psalmist wrote, 'Be still and know that I am God…'

Get Out of Jail Card

"A key part of forgiveness is to see the gift in the encounter and be authentically grateful."

Russell Sturgess

chapter 6

Being pardoned

While you are in jail with your life sentence, you develop various skills and abilities, which enable you to avoid your core fear. In my case, I became a very skilled healer bringing relief from pain for thousands of people. As a very competent educator and public speaker I was able to bring useful knowledge and understanding to thousands of people. My love for food allowed me to prepare beautiful meals, which I have shared with family and friends on many occasions, and having observed women at close quarters, I gained an enriched appreciation of the nature and qualities of women and the feminine.

I also developed the skill for creating training programs, including the Enhances Awareness Program (EAP), a mentoring tool designed to help people free themselves from their life sentence. So, for all of the challenges my life sentence brought, it also brought me and others many gifts. There is a Christian scripture, which, when paraphrased, says we are given weaknesses that they would become our strengths.

A whole of life perspective

I'm inviting you to take a holistic perspective on your jail time and life sentence rather than seeing it only as a handicap. What if you chose the circumstances into which you were

Being pardoned

born? Your parents, your position in the family, your health challenges and experiences, how you were raised? What if you chose these experiences because you wanted to expand your consciousness as a spiritual being? What if, rather than a physical being having a spiritual experience, you are a spiritual being having a physical experience? What if your life sentence was a Divine gift given solely for the purpose of expanding your awareness? Instead of feeling shame or regret for the things you have done, what if you were able to be truly grateful? The ability to see your experience differently, is essential if you are to be completely pardoned from your life sentence.

Self-forgiveness is the key to finding stillness and release from your jail. In this context, forgiveness is defined as selective remembering — choosing to reflect back on an experience and being able to see it as beneficial. You can learn to see the gift in your imprisonment if you selectively remember your life sentence. Forgiveness is complete once you can express gratitude for your incarceration.

If you created a CV that focused on the abilities and understanding that has arisen out of your life sentence, others would look at it, and speak in glowing terms about your accomplishments and abilities. It is likely that you have developed some amazing talents and have emerged as a unique individual. Being able to acknowledge those attributes, requires the scrutiny of an aware adult, not a wounded child.

Put away childish things

While we are in jail, our consciousness (how we think, feel, sense and desire) is aligned with our childhood story and, by default, we only listen to our seven-year-old self. The truth is, if we had seen ourselves as others see us sooner, we may have stopped listening to the inner child sooner.

I invite you to take time to write your CV about what you have achieved, and the skills you have developed while serving out your sentence. Go and do this right now. Then answer the following questions.

How do you feel when you read about the good stuff that emerged from your life sentence?

If you saw someone else with these attributes and achievements, what would you think of them?

Can you see yourself in the same light?

'When I was a child, I spoke as a child, I understood as a child, I thought as a child: but when I became a man, I put away childish things' (1 Corinthians 13:11). This is the time to

Being pardoned

put away childish things — the needs that arose out of your life sentence.

The evidence of awareness

Maintaining an enhanced level of awareness allows you to be more present to each instant, more mindful and free from your life sentence. You will know you are free when you stop reacting negatively to the difficulties and challenges that inadvertently turn up throughout life. When you are in your story, these triggers become a drama that typically results in some form of suffering. When you are free from your story, you are free from the drama. As you become more aware of the story and aware of a more self-loving alternative, you can choose to be mindful in each moment. You realise that you don't have to live life habitually.

There is a tipping-point in the commitment to being more aware and more mindful, where the path of least resistance sees you naturally aligning with a more self-loving alternative to your less serving old habits. The more self-compassionate you become, the more compassion you show to others, indicating you are free of your life sentence.

Lastly, you are free when you embrace a Divinely inspired purpose and declare, 'Not my will, but Divine Will'. At this juncture, you commit to hearing and responding to the prompts of the Still Small Voice.

When you are more mindful, your values become clearer. While imprisoned by your life sentence, what you valued was driven by the needs that arose from your story. Your values were focused on avoiding your core fear. Many of us fear being perceived as having no worth. In my case, my story was my need to be noticed. I feared that I could be overlooked. So, I put all of my resources, time and talent into being noticed. The Catch 22 in all of this is that, even if I had received all of the attention I wanted, I still wouldn't have believed I was deserving, because I was only listening to the voice of the seven-year-old. This scenario was destined to result in unhappy relationships, depression, obesity and bankruptcy.

When you make the transition from your life sentence and self-imposed incarceration, to awareness and mindfulness, your values change. Wealth, power and popularity are replaced with social justice, mercy and unconditional love. Survival and scarcity are replaced by service and abundance. Most notably, your experience of life changes. People observing you will notice that you are less stressed and appear to be genuinely happy. They see that you are

Being pardoned

less isolated and act in ways that are genuinely engaging. You have clarity about your direction and purpose. You have more energy and are more involved in life. Friends will see you making changes in the way you live your life. Changes that inspire you to push the boundaries; to experience the new; and to let go of your old limiting beliefs and attitudes.

If the drama makes your life exciting, you may think a life of inner peace and stillness will be boring. I guess if you find living a meaningful life with clarity of purpose, almost no stress, greatly improved health and constantly experiencing unconditional love, (not to mention a wonderful sense of your worth), boring, you could be excused for opting for staying in jail.

So what will a life with new values look like?

Social justice

With an expanded awareness of yourself and the world around you, one of the first noticeable changes is an expanded ability to see opportunities where you can be of assistance to others. Of course, having also developed an expanded sense of your own worth, you will only act on these opportunities in ways that reflect the love you have, first and foremost, for yourself.

I refer to this ability to see and act for the wellbeing of others as social justice. It is a term broad enough to also include looking after the planet and its critters. When you are free, the motive arises from genuine compassion, rather than due to your story. It's important to determine if you are being motivated by how it serves you, or others. Mother Teresa made the observation that she didn't care about what people did, but why they did it. Love or fear?

Mercy

Because you have been able to apply forgiveness to yourself, you will be naturally inclined to be more merciful to others. You will understand that your life sentence was not so much an imprisonment as it was an apprenticeship. In the first chapter, I shared the childhood story of Linda, the daughter of missionaries. Linda, over many years, had done a lot of healing and personal development work, but she still remained in her prison. Her fear was palpable. When she was able to clearly identify her life sentence, and describe the nature of her story, she was in a position to see its gift. Then she was able to express authentic gratitude for what she had been through.

I was amazed with two observations that Linda made, following her reframing of the trauma that had occurred in her childhood. Firstly, she explained that, given how dynamic the gifts were that she had received, she wouldn't change the trauma she had experienced. This is a woman who had lived under the fear of molestation and abuse her whole life.

Her next statement was also truly amazing. Linda said that being on the outside of jail, and looking back on her life sentence, was like reading a newspaper report on someone else's story. It was as if she had become disassociated from her past. Many people who go through the Enhances Awareness Program experience much the same thing. It's as if their past belongs to someone else. After almost 45 years, Linda was in a place of regular stillness.

As an extension to this awakening, she has been able to forgive her abusers. That is extraordinary. She has learnt to 'selectively remember' her life sentence, and thereby extend mercy to others. If stillness is your priority, mercy becomes your primary function. This is the second new value that you embrace.

Charity

Linda's transformation, and release from her story, naturally ushered her towards the third new value that she integrated into her awareness, charity. Charity is a love that seeks to help others find a pardon from their own life sentence. Linda has taken the gifts that she obtained through her imprisonment and is using them to help others in similar circumstances.

Through her expanded awareness, Linda has removed the filters of fear and victimhood that distorted every encounter she had with people misusing power. Now she is no longer sympathetic, but empathetic. Sympathy disempowers, empathy empowers. Linda is now able to identify the difference between form and content, and brings her gifts of healing to anyone, male or female, who is imprisoned in a life sentence of victimhood.

Abuse of power can take many forms and, by rising above her story, Linda's capacity to help others is now very broad.

Peacemaker

The final value is that of a peacemaker. The peacemaker is the person who sees divine order in everything, in every extreme or duality. Good and bad, right and wrong, all of the possibilities of opposites are understood to be divinely ordered. Having embraced the values of justice, mercy and charity, the peacemaker has witnessed it all and

Being pardoned

knows that there isn't anything under heaven which does not have a divine purpose. Armed with that understanding, the peacemaker knows that everything serves, and can maintain their stillness as a result. The peacemakers only function is to be mindful, and his or her primary priority is inner stillness.

Living life with purpose

Since I have shared the journey thus far from my own personal experience, I guess it is appropriate that I describe how my life has unfolded since being pardoned.

Relationships

I have several key relationship dynamics in my life. Let me begin by explaining the nature of relationship that I have with my ex-partner. Until just very recently, we were still working together. We saw each other every working day of the week, as she worked in the office next to me. There is still a strong feeling of love between us. However, it's a love that is no longer bound to the needs that arose respectively from our stories. It's a love that honours each other's purpose and vision. All the angst that regularly surfaced throughout our life-partnership has gone.

Get Out of Jail Card

My relationship with my family, including my ex-wife, four children, respective partners and my grandson, has become more engaged and fulfilling. Regular family gatherings are now common. There are family meals and days of family activity filled with fun, laughter and joy. There is more space for love, sharing, helping and caring. My ex-wife and her new husband are welcome in my home, as I am in theirs. This means that we can still function as a family, albeit in a whole different form.

As previously discussed, my youngest daughter was suddenly confronted with a challenging mental health issue a few years ago. The speed with which it appeared took us all by surprise. Without any hesitation, my other three children, my ex-wife and I took a week off and hired a large apartment in a local resort where we cohabitated for a week. It gave us a chance to embrace my youngest child in a united family environment.

Once I was sure of my vision and purpose, I was confident that I was free of my imprisonment. My weight stabilised, I was no longer depressed — in fact I was fully committed to, and engaged in, my calling and purpose. I was a long way down the path of stabilising my finances and I no longer needed to be in a relationship, as I had found the love I needed within.

Being pardoned

With my daughter's mental illness, I had resolved that I would take on the role as her primary carer. Between my enhanced commitment to my purpose and my parenting-role life was full and rewarding. Although it presented many challenges, I had found my place of stillness (most of the time).

During this time, I met a woman with whom I am now in relationship. It is a mindful relationship, one where we are both aware of our stories. I have never had one of these before. In those rare occasions we find ourselves at variance with each other, we immediately identify how our respective stories are involved, and practice being mindful in how we resolve it.

Mindfulness and compassion have become the two most important qualities to bring to our relationship. They allow me to remain true to my calling and purpose. As we share a similar vision and purpose and these sit as the foundation to our relationship. Our personal fulfilment is met in our calling and not in each other. There is no trade agreement, only a mutual commitment to a mutual purpose.

I am blessed that I now receive love that tops up the love I feel for myself. Imagine — no arguments, no fear of judgement or rejection, a shared purpose, the ability to live in the now, soulful intimacy, joy and gratitude.

Career

My career is the platform for my calling, purpose and vision. I am working full-time on fulfilling the commitment I made several years ago on that wet, windy cape in the northwest of Spain. Prior to the Camino, I was inspired to create the Enhances Awareness Program (see eapmentor.com). Since being pardoned from my life sentence, I continue to use the gifts I was given during my sentence to expand and enrich EAP.

When you are on the right path, you experience Divine Flow — a sense of effortlessness. It is evidence that you are free of your story. Each day, my work guides people to find balance, freedom, clarity, health and joy in their lives through gaining a deep sense of their worth. I couldn't imagine doing anything more fulfilling and rewarding.

Not only that, I am now training other people to do the same work. Currently, at any one time, there can be 50 people going through EAP, improving their lives. This program guides people to live life mindfully, by helping them to be free of their life sentence.

Each week I am privileged to observe firsthand the magic of transformation as suffering disappears from people's lives. I hear the joy that other EAP mentors express as they

Being pardoned

too help facilitate lasting changes in the lives of the people they work with. Each day I am filled with joy and gratitude in my work. Each day I go home fulfilled.

Abundance

I have enjoyed times of great abundance throughout my life. But when I was fully caught up in my story, my world came tumbling down. The result of that was divorce, depression and bankruptcy. In his teachings, Jesus said, "By their fruits you will know them". Obviously, the fruits of divorce, depression and bankruptcy were evidence of the unsustainable nature of living life within my story. In 2013, I began to fully understand my life sentence and the prison that I had built for myself. It took two years for the healing to be fully expressed and, now, I am clearly witnessing the fruits of living my life mindfully.

I am in a loving, compassionate relationship. I am engaged in my calling and purpose through my work in EAP. I am 56 kilograms lighter than my heaviest weight. By living my life mindfully through, being more aware and being free from story, my world is filled with joy, peace and love.

Staying mindful is the 'Get Out of Jail' card that will never see me in jail again.

Get Out of Jail Card

"The only thing capable of changing the epidemic of lifestyle disease, are the changes made in the mind and heart of each individual. Each person will have to be inspired to desire to make the change as an act of self-love."

Russell Sturgess

Afterword

About EAP

Get Out of Jail Card

The Enhances Awareness Program

(eapmentor.com)

Russell Sturgess is the founder and principal of EAP Mentor. There are three mindfulness products that are intrinsic to the business:

Enhances Awareness Program (EAP) is a weekly personal mentoring program that runs for up to 12 months. The structured program enhances all aspects of awareness to help participants naturally achieve a mindful approach to life.

Pathways to Mindfulness is a two-day workshop or one-on-one mentoring program that focuses on the roles that people have in their work lives that are causing burnout, compassion fatigue, anxiety and unmanageable stress. It is oriented to health professionals, business professionals and teachers.

Be a Mentor is an opportunity for anyone wanting to make a difference in the world through guiding people to live more mindfully. EAP Mentor runs regular training programs to qualify people to become an EAP Mentor.

Please visit the eapmentor.com website to find out more about EAP. You can also see regular mindfulness tips on our Facebook Page @eapmentor.

About EAP

What participants have said about the Enhances Awareness Program.

"My journey with the Enhances Awareness Program (EAP) has been surprising. Despite having participated in numerous self-development programs over the last 30 years, as well as training and working both as a counsellor and coach, I was drawn to EAP after seeing friends I respected experience great benefits. Initially, I expected to be reminded of what I already knew, but soon realised that the apparent simplicity of the structure belied the depth of the work. In time, the awareness that I developed enabled me to clearly see, and almost effortlessly change, some core patterns I had been battling with for years! I wholeheartedly recommend this life-changing program to anyone wanting to transform and enrich their life."

Jane Hoffmann Davies
mNZAC, mNZAB, mIMNZ

"I write from my position as a medical specialist and also an international healthcare leader, having been an advisor to the NZ government and the WHO (World Health Organisation), and also as the cofounder of an international movement for compassionate healthcare, Hearts in Healthcare. Together with my wife, Meredith, we did the full Enhances Awareness Program with EAP Mentor (Russell), which involves many months of one-on-one weekly mentoring sessions and a highly structured program. Both of us realised considerable benefits in both our professional and personal lives as a result of this program, which I highly recommend. The program is based on a great depth of knowledge and wisdom and the learning resources are truly excellent. Of all the many programs in self-development I have undertaken, the EAP Mentor program would rank among the most valuable.

I have also attended the introductory, two-day 'Aware Health Professional' program and am happy to endorse this product also. In fact, I believe this program to be so valuable that I have offered to help revise and adapt the program to suit the specific needs of physicians, as a 'thank you' gift to EAP Mentor."

Dr Robin Youngson, MA MbChB FANZCA
Anaesthetic Specialist
Cofounder of Hearts in Healthcare

www.ingramcontent.com/pod-product-compliance
Lightning Source LLC
Chambersburg PA
CBHW040325300426
44112CB00021B/2876